Keijiro Suga

TRANSIT BLUES

Keijiro Suga
TRANSIT BLUES

IPSI CHAPBOOK 16

University of Canberra
International Poetry Studies Institute
Series editor: Paul Munden

Transit Blues
Second edition
IPSI with Recent Work Press
Canberra, Australia

Copyright © Keijiro Suga, 2018

ISBN: 978-0-6486853-2-6 (paperback)

First published 2018, this edition 2019
International Poetry Studies Institute
Faculty of Arts and Design
University of Canberra
Canberra, Australia
http://ipsi.org.au

All rights reserved. This book is copyright. Except for private study, research, criticism or reviews as permitted under the Copyright Act, no part of this book may be reproduced, stored in a retrieval system, or transmitted in any form by any means without prior written permission. Enquiries should be addressed to the publisher.

Design by Caren Florance

CONTENTS

Walking as a Prayer	1
Transit Blues	2
The Crow Poems	6
In the Country Where December is in Midsummer	10
The Origin of the Sleep Dance	12
On Migration	14
From *Waves of Absence*	20
The Silent Raven	23
My Dog Papyrus	25
Acknowledgements	27
About the poet	29

WALKING AS A PRAYER

'Walking itself has a value as a prayer,'
Children of that tribe are taught this from the youngest age.
Indeed, they do walk a lot.
Stepping on fixed points every day,
They make their daily pilgrimages in their land without territory.
They call the names of grasses and flowers,
They touch the trees with their hands,
And notice the flights of birds and the movements of insects
That they perceive only in the corner of their visual field.
At each point they have a distinctive object of prayer.
Here, it is land, the material basis that supports life.
Here, it is water, shaping the movement by its flow and circulation.
Here, it is fire, which gives heat to the world and dries every life.
Here, it is wind, the ultimate secret of being that closely resembles nothing.
In this way the land has become their altar.
Their walking becomes a form of prayer.

TRANSIT BLUES

Transit. I'm in transit.
Sitting in a train that doesn't even run.
Like a hobo *sin rumbo*. Without direction.

Transition. My perception is in transition.
My position on the ghost train in the sky
Is a juxtaposition of my forgotten past and my foretold future.

'The blues has always been a migratory music' (Charles Keil).
Your position and transposition urge translation.
Translations occur as proofs of distance.
A migrant's song can only be the blues.
Sing the blues in the bluest lights of Yokohama, California.

'I walk ten miles every night,' boasted a friend of mine.
'I will walk around a single tree a million times during my lifetime,'
    I answered.

Anchored to a single tree,
It is enough to experience many dawns and sunsets of the earth.
Then this Asian island city in which you live
Is again, before your eyes transformed into jungles, steppes, tundra,
    and deserts.

'Tabi ni yamite / yume wa kareno o / kake meguru' (Basho)

> Falling ill on a journey
> My dream takes me over and through
> Desolate fields.

This dream journey has been going on since the moment you began.
Falling ill on a journey also means
Journey is the illness.

Standing on the pavement where each night the carnival takes place,
Calling back the empty, desolate field to that spot.
Covered streams once again become turbulent overflowing rivers.
The fish and turtles hiding at the bottom of time
Take off swimming all at once.

This city always seems to be moving through something.
This city is always on the journey toward its opposite.
'It is a city made only of exceptions, exclusions, incongruities,
    contradictions.' (Italo Calvino)

One day thirty years ago
In the transit zone of Honolulu International Airport
I sat down and thought about which direction to take
To Seattle or to Auckland (Tamaki Makaurau)?
To the village that bears the name of Chief Seattle
Where the Coastal Salish people catch salmon?
Or to the huge fish of the Maori people
Dragged out of the Pacific by Trickster Maui?

Between Americas and Oceania
Between North and South
Between the ocean and islands
Between local native worlds and the global market of late capitalism
Which direction should I choose to go in?

Wherever you go the sky and the meteor follow you.
The sea and dolphins duplicate you.
All around you, *es el huracán*. It's a hurricane.
The wind is powerful enough to help your transmigration.
Then my friend the philosopher says:
'Earth, water, fire, and wind, these are called *stoicheia* in Greek and
    elementa in Latin.

Flowers are the elements of nature.
Being also attracts mind like flowers.
People live, enveloped by being.
Just like they sleep in the coffin enveloped by flowers.'
   (Shiro Yamauchi)

Poetry is a desire to be everywhere at once.
Poetry is a desire to inhabit every letter in the world.
Motionless transformation takes place in the nest of migrant swallows.
Timeless transaction takes place in the mind of sun-struck sparrows.

And my friend the philosopher says:
'We gather mountain plants, various mushrooms and nuts,
We hunt bears and rabbits to sell them in small numbers to earn cash.
At the beginning of April we usually run out of food
By then we've eaten all the pickled vegetables; what's left is
Too sour from fermentation.
As a child I always felt
The coming of Spring as heavy and sad.' (Shiro Yamauchi)

My song is a song of the strangely wicked wolf.
The wickedness of the wolf consists in slowing down the time
That flows in our veins.

Transit in action.
Estamos viajando para vivir.
J'adore les bruits de la lumière.
I respect the thoughtfulness of small creatures.

Then my philosopher friend says:
'I am but a voice or light surfacing from the horizon of the non-person
Well before the first-person

I appear when I feel the light that is not me as mine
I'd like to believe in the Scottishness of Duns Scotus.'

My mind is transient.
My words are intermittent.
My vision is often blurred.
My voice resembles a silence.

Then my philosopher friend says:
'What is the origin of I?
Leaves of trees and grass are organs to feel the wind
Why does my heart move when the wind blows?
Isn't that because I, too, am wind?' (Shiro Yamauchi)

All around, *es mayo que canta*.
Pour féliciter la naissance de Karl Marx d'il y a deux cent ans.
Carlito was born on the 5th of May, you know,
Which happens to be a national holiday in Japan
Called Children's Day.
Be united, children of the world with other-than-human.
With the mountains, rivers, grass, trees, birds, beasts, bugs, and fish.

'Harukaze ya / tsustumi nagoshite / ie tooshi' (Buson)

> Spring breeze
> Long is the bank of the river
> Home is far.

Do you hear me?
Do you hear me?
This is my Transit Blues.

THE CROW POEMS

1

The crow is watching your every move.
Watching how you look at the flowers and touch their petals.
The sakura will be over soon, spring will deepen;
Tulips begin blossoming with anti-oxidant colours.
Flowers aim at the light and become transparent in the light.
The crow, too, is looking at the penetrating light.
The crow is also looking at your helpless mind,
Watching how you look up at the sky and follow the drifting clouds.
Bits of clouds deploy multiple white shapes.
Each piece cut out and flies like a bird.
The sky is always one; it cannot fragment
Yet you hear the songs and the birds are generated by the sound.
The crow is never surprised no matter what happens.
The crow never laughs no matter what it sees.
But the crow observes everything closely
And reports to you what it registered in its memory.

2

'Say, can I eat this?' asks the crow.
About the corn cobs
And the seeds and rinds of the watermelon you have discarded.
When summer begins and strong light produces heat
The crow's feathers turn as black as the universe.
Consider well the relations between flight and cooling.
'Maybe I can come along,' says the crow as if talking to itself.
Like a dog, it just sensed that you were about to leave.
'You can go as far as you like. I don't mind. The topology of the globe prevents mazes. Doesn't matter which direction you go.'
The crow's a jolly fellow traveller, a reliable companion,
Because the crow never expects anything.
The crow never desires anything, even what there is too much of.
The crow never abandons whatever is necessary.
Then the crow, with blood boiling,
Traces a straight line into infinity across the capricious sky.

3

The crow welcomes autumn with precision.
This is the season when life changes gears
And shifts from combustion to preservation.
Gee, I must have picked up some weight; don't you laugh.
Merry sparrows enjoy their happy harvest festival.
Stubborn snails are about to hide themselves.
The crow doesn't lament autumn, nor sings praise to it.
If you head towards the mountains he will keep you company.
If you look for mushrooms he will help you.
All matter is dreams given shape.
The contingencies of the non-material world
Only appear that way, under a certain light.
The crow doesn't care if his body is but a dream.
The crow is calm, even if his senses are patterns of waves.
He controls his blood-sugar levels in anticipation of flight,
Even if that is nothing more than the shadow of a dream called flight.

4

If you want to know the truth, the crow loves winter.
In big cities, no worries about the scarcity of food.
And he loves snow, hopes to get as much snow as possible.
On the ever-renewing surface of the timeless whiteness
He thinks of transforming himself into a hieroglyph
By pulling out a feather or two.
'Oh, crown, crow, my credo is cruciferous!'
Like a nail driving this cross-shaped credo into his heart
He hums his own song deep in his throat, 'cr, cr,'
I am a crown with no ornaments to relativise the human world.
My eyes are portable nights tinted jet-black.
It's the blackness in which all hopes melt into blue.
When your world brightens up and becomes pure white,
By flying over the surface of the earth innocently purified
I will show you the ultimate unity of black, white, and light.
This is it, my golden tail and my two wings gleaming in gold.

IN THE COUNTRY WHERE DECEMBER IS IN MIDSUMMER

In the country where December is in midsummer
Santa Claus is a Teddy Bear.
He uses a chocolate-coloured Labrador for a reindeer
So he can sleigh through the withered grasslands.
Teddy Bear's work is to collect gifts.
Just as there is anti-gravity for gravity
All gifts call for anti-gifts.
After 'I want this, I want that,' turns into 'not really,'
Once you are actually given what you wanted,
Gifts lie dormant in your rooms.
The Animal Santa retrieves them and sends them back to heaven
So you can become lighter than speech balloons
And less afraid of the unknown and even of death.
When your heart clears up
The atmospheric pressure rises accordingly
Blowing away the sheep and clouds
And the sky becomes blue expanse.
The universe also clears up.
Now my blue Stratocaster can
Cast pebble-like notes up into the stratosphere.
Listen! I'm playing this for my animal Santa
From the vibrating strings, at each moment

Departs an invisible arrow
To hit the evil,
To hit demons.
And when struck by the arrow
Dead birds come hurriedly back to life
And take to flight once again with good humour.
That's Teddy Bear's victory.
That's Labrador's glory.
That's our Christmas prayer.
That's the best possible gift we have for the world.

THE ORIGIN OF THE SLEEP DANCE

All your friends in the air are sleeping in the mysterious green ray.
All your friends under the ground are awake in the swinging darkness.
And you, little you, sleeping on the surface of the earth on a grass bed
Have a nightmare under the scent of jasmine emitted by the Moon.
Sleeping people make a gear-like circle in the air.
People who are awake communicate with each other silently in the ground.
You, in your sleep, mimic a dog's long howl
Asking for help to the dogs of the last century.
I whisper quietly into your ear.
(A snap of the fingers to cut out the air.)
(With your whistle cause a wind that blows up the slope of the mountain.)
A shining melody runs on the surface of the river like a pororoca.
The problem is probably all about your self-definition.
Your self is compartmentalised like a beehive, you say.
Still, four colours are enough to paint them separately.
(You tend to make things more complicated than they really are, don't you?)
Your friends on the shore are all sleeping among the trees.
Your inland friends think it's a good time to migrate.
On the deserted surface of the earth now you are attempting
An intrusion in the dream of a friend who is really sleeping.
A re-encounter somewhere with a friend who incessantly texts you.
When for that purpose you stand up asleep

A transformation of landforms begins inside your body.
Erosion, deposition, eruption, and landslides
Volcanic ash falls on your sleeping friends like snow.
And the friends already walking begin their awkward dance
That awakens the friends sleeping in the air.
And the friends under the ground come out of the ground
And begin to dance vigorously as if to regain their pasts.
You dance, too, asleep and loose, with an inevitable African taste
In a batik dress and a turban that becomes you.
All these scenes I am photographing with my iPhone.
Look, here is a snapshot I took of you dancing.

ON MIGRATION

A chocolate-coloured girl on a chocolate-coloured bicycle
Goes round and round a solitary standing man.
Like the bubble-net feeding of a pod of humpback whales
She tightens a circle into a spiral in this empty town plaza.
Is she a predator or a playful dolphin?
This happens because I'm standing still like a stone Buddha, he thinks.
He decides to sit down on the stone wall of the plaza.
This plaza, where there is no temple, no church, no statue, no scarecrow,
Is now flooded with rose-pink sunlight from a late-afternoon sun,
And children without shadows are playing, beyond life and death.
The standing man with an unfamiliar face is me.
I just know it.
The girl suddenly puts away the bicycle
When she folds it in two
It fits nicely on her back.
I was surprised to see such a triumph of industrial design.
Looking closer, it is in fact not a bicycle at all.
It looks like some kind of mammal, a simian perhaps
But as it looks content playing the role of a vehicle
I don't dare say anything.
Then the girl and I talk about migration.
She is in her early teens, standing with her arms crossed in front of me.
She is so keen on finding out the rent of my apartment.
I was thinking that this must be somewhere in the Bengali region.
But as it turns out it is a small, remote city somewhere in Japan.
Nothing frivolous, the atmosphere is calm and warm.
'As I need to seriously concentrate on my study
I prefer a town where I can live safely and securely.'

How about Takamatsu or Kochi, I suggested.
'But the pine trees are too crooked, aren't they?
And what exactly do you mean by High Knowledge?'
I explain to her that Japanese place names don't always reflect reality.
Takamatsu is a land of large rocks and man-made ponds,
Kochi is known for a school of bonito flying over high waves,
Goto archipelago is famous for Polynesian canoes and *Doctrina Christã*,
Cape Sata draws your soul to an atlas
By its extraordinary landform.
'All I want to know is if it's a nice town to live in
Without discrimination of religion and language,' says the girl.
The *ura* in Saiki is quite similar to small Caribbean bays.
Sasebo comes from the French expression: *Ça, c'est beau!*
The girl is certainly of Indian origin, but by then, somehow
I know she's an Indian girl from France's overseas region of
    Guadeloupe.
'So the best places are in Shikoku and Kyushu, like everybody says.'
The names of Odate, Misawa, and Nemuro cross my mind.
But I know too little about these cities to have a clear image.
(A large yellow dog, Americans jogging on the beach, the wetland
    and a runway.)
I want a path where I can walk for a long time, I want natural coasts
    and rivers,
I tell her my wishes but this way we don't know
Anymore for whom we are choosing a place.
Casually it came to mind and I asked her: Do you have a passport?
She glared at me, saying, 'Is that a proper question?'
I sort of regretted that I asked.
Before I knew it the monkey on the back of the girl became a dog,
And is now sleeping soundly on her lap.

This is such a peaceful moment but somewhere
Anxiety pierces me from inside.
Now I need to go,
But where to?
Suddenly a kind voice addressed me: 'I'll give you a lift.'
This must be the girl's father but such a young father he is.
If she is, say, thirteen, the man looks still in his twenties
Wearing a nice pink shirt and all smiles.
'Japanese is easy to speak but I don't have time to learn the characters,'
He said, showing me his little notebook.
It seemed he wrote Japanese in some Indian script.
It's so kind of him to offer me a lift but I don't know where I should go.
The man has a bright red, remodeled pickup.
Shall we go there, then, that island where they catch flying fish?
'Oh, all right, in that case we'll leave the car and walk,' he said.
And we walked on the single-track railroad
Until the rail tracks came to a strait.
I can see the turquoise surface of the turbulent sea in the bright
    sunshine.
I see swirls, and numerous white heads of waves.
The rails have wooden sleepers but the spaces between them are
    unbelievably wide.
Should you fall, it's sixty metres straight into the ocean.
I try to step, timidly and cautiously, from one bar to another.
Then the girl tells me: 'Don't go like that, it's easier to walk on the
    iron rail.'
So we walk on the iron rails, me on the right side
The girl on the left, parallel to each other.
The wind is strong; it blows up my hair and I can't keep myself from
    laughing.

At each step I know I may fall but I am not afraid anymore.
The rails, parallel, get narrower until they are only as wide as a regular ladder.
So the girl goes first and we walk in Indian file.
Soon we come to the island on the other side and there is nothing to make one uneasy.
There is absolutely no evil in the air.
Wild goats climb the steep slopes of the cliff with ease.
Look, that's *pinza*, *hija*, I cry out.*
The father and daughter laugh happily, saying, 'Haven't you seen one before?'
There are many goats.
It would be nice to live on an island like this.
There, goat catchers donning lifelines wear the hunted goats around their neck.
Once you ascend the narrow path on the rocky surface to the top,
You see the island really is a caldera with its centre caved in.
Near the middle of the island stands an ugly figure of a woman
And there was a notice, saying: 'As there was no goddess on this island
We made it ourselves.'
'A culture without a goddess is too lonely,' says the girl's father.
'As I don't have a mother,
I will make one myself,' says the girl.
The father looked sad to hear that.
Because of the strong current the coast of this island collects
Many dead bodies and oval squids and live goats.
Thus were established gods, local specialties, and the hero of the eco-system.
I, who don't believe in any god,
Am disturbed by the real presence of this spooky goddess statue

And my knees feel wobbly.
That also weakens my eyes and at the same time
I begin to see many different spirits in their transparent blue contours.
The sky gets darker and darker and the clouds are swiftly moving.
'Was my mother a goat or a wild pig or a dolphin?'
The girl pronounces clearly with her chocolate-coloured lips.
Hearing that I wondered if my own mother was
A stone statue or a stone woman or the daughter of a stone mason.
Of course this is no more than a baseless legend.
It's an illusion if the air looks like the colours of the rainbow.
I notice the grains of Indian corn dropped on the ground making a thread.
If you follow them you will surely arrive somewhere.
I wish the weather would change like the seasons change.
That's the best way to accelerate your life.
But the animals, they don't care about humans' illusions.
Their seasonal strategies for survival
Teach me that the human mind was a form of biological adaptation.
Try to survive without using your mind; or
Try to survive by maximising your mind.
From here spreads a grassland covered with thickets
Continuing softly to the shore on the other side.
'Look, there's a whale!'
The dogs of the island are ceremoniously barking
At the coastal whale that strayed into the bay.
'The whales come to pray to the goddess of the island,' says a local lady.
But I don't believe what she says.
I look up and there are raptors gliding through the air
Catching the fish that followed the whale and landed on the beach
In an abrupt descent one after the other.

Oh, what a great view! What a nice thing I witnessed!
I am filled with unexpected joy.
The wharf and the surrounding areas are neatly covered in concrete.
So the girl takes out that monkey bicycle and begins to ride.
'I'll go round and round, winding back time,' she says.
The sky turns into a tender, pale blue and a calm dusk has returned.
It's not bad to live by the bay like this.
It's not bad for thinking about natural history.
It's not bad for restraining the roaming of the mind.
'We had a whale of time today!' I yelled to the father and daughter.
The girl is running round and round her father and me.
'Look, Daddy, I go round and round, I'll rewind time.'
The whale spouted, making a big, resounding sound.
'Look, Daddy, that's Mother,' she says.
And when I look there is a chocolate-coloured woman riding the back of the whale
Waving at us.
And when I look the young father is all smiles
His cheeks wet with tears.

*Pinza ('goat' in the Tokara archipelago), *hija* ('goat' in the Ryukyus)

FROM *WAVES OF ABSENCE*

2

In the town where people have disappeared,
On the wasteland where the town has disappeared,
In this vast area littered with rubble,
A dog is running, on its self-assigned mission of patrol.
What the dog is aiming at is connecting heat in surviving lives.
He tries to connect somebody breathing and somebody blinking
And make them talk using unknown words.
But he does not meet anybody.
He stops once in a while, listens carefully, sniffs scents,
And starts running again, in the town where dwelling has
  been cancelled.
Running, the dog takes off its fur.
He thinks of putting it on someone to warm her up.
Then he stops and lets his hot urine gush out.
He is trying to mark his smell and life on the spot.
Wondering where all the people have gone,
The naked dog, out of his fur and covered with blood,
  is silently running.

5

The cows do not dare go beyond the fence.
They are not afraid of the wind's growl, not scared of the sea's roar.
It is just that the humans they know are no longer there,
So they feel nervous and they stay put.
Nearby, the marshes have thoroughly vanished.
The migratory birds no longer come around.
In the town, all the shops and temples are gone,
And the cats go on wandering, more than ever before.
On the hills, the horses are running around breathing fire
And the pigs have grown wings and are flying low in groups.
The raccoons and weasels have made their mass exodus.
Raptors and reptiles have not been sighted for a long time.
Only the cows would not leave this place.
Since they no longer have appetite, imaginary rumination is enough.
Will the faces of familiar people return tomorrow?
The haggard cows have waited fixedly for a hundred years already.

7

Seven ravens are standing on this deserted shore.
Here was a town until yesterday.
Deserted, but also filled with light,
And full of innocence that was never before experienced.
The snowflakes on their black feathers are gradually melting,
Becoming little drops of light.
Temporarily abandoning the sky where the restless crows
And seagulls are noisily circling,
Seven ravens are watching over the shore.
Because there are beings travelling on the shore.
They are numberless, but neither a group nor a flock,
One by one, one by one,
They cross the cold water,
Being washed by the beautiful light
Pouring down from between the dark clouds.
The ravens are silently watching their departure.

THE SILENT RAVEN

The raven is nostalgic for whiteness.
Which was its original colour.
Before it chattered a bit too much
And its snowy white turned to pure shadow.
Not a metamorphosis, really,
Since the form remained the same.
So what might you say, my classicist,
Metapigmentation or something?
At least it's not a case of metempsychosis
Or the sad psychosis of some of its descendants.
The raven, or the crow, too,
Might have yearned for peacock-like eyes on its wings
That could peer into the secrets
Of the multidimensional universe.
But in reality, for no logical reason,
White went black and the world became unfair.
But that world is only Greco-Roman, you know.
In the northern myth of another continent
The raven, cultural hero, brought light to this world
And was at once human and bird.
I go with the ravens and crows.
Honestly, this black-and-white argument is quite
Moot. If you knew how to look at
Their true colour, it's blue.
A blue that transcends night and day,
The old world and the new world,
Life and afterlife.
That's the colour of the sky

And the raven embodies
The fate of the Earth and its atmospheric coating.
This much I learned, *meu deus*, I'd better stop my chattering.
But let me add one thing: there's another angle to this question.
A true synthesis of black and white is already accomplished
By the magpie. It steals.
A meta-raven, a meta-crow, it globalises myth with its real-life action.
Pied and always on the go,
Aggressive yet very funny,
My cultural hero, my previous and after-life!

MY DOG PAPYRUS

When I was a child I had a dog
We called him Papyrus, brindle-coloured,
At my heels everywhere I went.
In early spring, it was the black soil
Lightly covered in snow, under our feet.
The wind blew so cold we feared our ears might shear off.
I shouted, 'We are the wintering party!'
Papyrus just gave me an amused look.
His ears standing like those of a wolf
His tail coiled like a tornado
His eyes sharp as light.
A half a century ago roundworms killed him.

Last summer in Ayutthaya, Thailand
I was sitting under a tree, tired after my walk
When an ochre-coloured dog quietly approached
And sat gently by my side.
His muzzle sleek and black
I scratched him behind his ears.
His eyes narrowed, he seemed to smile
I called to him, 'Papyrus'
And he languidly wagged his tail.

> I'm waiting, you know, for you
> At the foot of that mountain
> When you head off towards its summit
> I'll keep you company
> Papyrus here
> All the things you hold within you
> All the things you have forgotten
> Papyrus will remember.

ACKNOWLEDGEMENTS

'Walking as a Prayer' was first published as number 'LI' in *The Rain Falling on the Sea*, 2012. Translated by the author.

'Transit Blues' was written for the symposium at the University of Trier, Germany, May 2018. Translated by the author.

'The Crow Poems', *'Ciencia en flores'*, 'In the Country Where December is Midsummer', 'The Origin of the Sleep Dance' are from *Numbers and Twilight*, 2017. Translated by the author with Doug Slaymaker.

'On Migration' is also from *Numbers and Twilight*, 2017. Translated by the author.

The three pieces of 'Waves of Absence' are from *Island Water, Island Fire*, 2011. Translated by the author with Doug Slaymaker.

'The Silent Raven' was written in English with some help from Forrest Gander for *Metamorphic: 21st Century Poets Respond to Ovid*, Nessa O'Mahony and Paul Munden (eds), Recent Work Press, 2017.

'My Dog Papyrus' was first published in Japanese in *The Yomiuri Shinbun*, 26 January 2018. Translated by the author with Doug Slaymaker.

Paul Munden kindly provided feedback on the manuscript and I have benefited considerably from his comments.

Keijiro Suga is a Tokyo-based poet and professor of critical theory at Meiji University. He is well known for his ten books of essays of which *Transversal Journeys* (2010) was awarded the Yomiuri Prize for Literature, one of the most prestigious literary awards in Japan. He is a prolific translator from French, English, and Spanish into Japanese in various disciplines. He has published four collections of poetry under the general title of *Agend'Ars*. A selection from this series is translated into Spanish and published in Mexico (Cuadrivio, 2015). His fifth collection, *Numbers and Twilight*, was published in December 2017.

IPSI: INTERNATIONAL POETRY STUDIES INSTITUTE

The International Poetry Studies Institute (IPSI) is part of the Centre for Creative and Cultural Research, Faculty of Arts and Design, University of Canberra. IPSI conducts research related to poetry, and publishes and promulgates the outcomes of this research internationally. The institute also publishes poetry and interviews with poets, as well as related material, from around the world. Publication of such material takes place in IPSI's online journal *Axon: Creative Explorations* (www.axonjournal.com.au) and through other publishing vehicles, such as Axon Elements. IPSI's goals include working – collaboratively, where possible – for the appreciation and understanding of poetry, poetic language and the cultural and social significance of poetry. The institute also organises symposia, seminars, readings and other poetry-related activities and events.

IPSI CHAPBOOK SERIES

The IPSI Chapbook Series publishes new work by leading poets from Australia and beyond, in limited editions. The chapbooks feature extended selections beyond the scope of most journals, highlighting innovative work by poets both new and well established, ahead of publication in book form. The series is linked to an international program of poets in residence at the University of Canberra.
Series Editor: Paul Munden.

CCCR: CENTRE FOR CREATIVE & CULTURAL RESEARCH

The Centre for Creative and Cultural Research (CCCR) is IPSI's umbrella organisation and brings together staff, adjuncts, research students and visiting fellows who work on key challenges within the cultural sector and creative field. A central feature of its research concerns the effects of digitisation and globalisation on cultural producers, whether individuals, communities or organisations.

www.ingramcontent.com/pod-product-compliance
Lightning Source LLC
Chambersburg PA
CBHW052309300426
44110CB00035B/2310